SOUL OF TOKYO

A GUIDE TO 30 EXCEPTIONAL EXPERIENCES

WRITTEN BY FANY AND AMANDINE PÉCHIODAT
CO-WRITTEN BY IWONKA BANCEREK
ILLUSTRATED BY KANAKO KUNO

JONGLEZ PUBLISHING

travel guides

"JAPAN TASTES
LIKE A GRAIN
OF RICE.

YOU HAVE TO BITE
INTO IT *GENTLY*.

AND GET
TO ITS HEART."

FRANÇOIS SIMON

WHAT YOU WON'T FIND
IN THIS GUIDE

- "Tokyo 101" from the city's tourist office
- the Japanese translation of "buy a subway ticket"
- what medications to bring

WHAT YOU WILL FIND
IN THIS GUIDE

- the ultimate cocktail
- a secret restaurant in Shibuya
- a teahouse hidden behind a flower shop
- the wildest onsen
- the best head massage
- the world's smallest bookstore
- the art of having standing sushi
- "Tokyo's Best Sushi 101"
- the Japanese translation of "taking a forest bath"

Because this guide isn't meant for first-time visitors to Tokyo, but for those who are coming back for another visit. Those who want to unlock its hidden doors, feel out its heartbeat, plumb every last nook and cranny to uncover its soul.

Having scoured the depths of Paris to share the city's best-kept secret spots, Fany and Amandine Péchiodat (the founders of My Little Paris, an influential newsletter-cum-lifestyle brand) now take on another city they love: Tokyo.

Five years ago, My Little Paris opened an office in Japan. And every time Fany lands in Tokyo, she takes advantage of being there to discover and try out new places. In 2018 she left My Little Paris to create the "Soul of" series with Thomas Jonglez, a new approach to traveling that captures a city's soul in 30 unforgettable experiences.

HOW THIS GUIDE **WORKS**

A CITY PUT UNDER THE MICROSCOPE

QUIRKY ENCOUNTERS
(with a tea master, creator of emotions, Michelin-starred chef/son of a geisha)

+

HUNDREDS OF PLACES TESTED

−

OVER-EXPOSED PLACES REJECTED

UNCHARTED SPOTS SNIFFED OUT

HUNDREDS OF PIECES OF SUSHI DEVOURED

GALLONS OF GREEN TEA SIPPED

A TOKYO-BORN-AND-BRED ILLUSTRATOR

MILES OF STREETS ROAMED

−

A FEW DEAD ENDS

=

The best 30 places in Tokyo

SYMBOLS USED IN "SOUL OF TOKYO"

< 40 euros

40 to 80 euros

> 80 euros

they don't speak English here, so ask your hotel (or a Japanese friend) to make a reservation

100% traditional Japan

even better for couples

you'll often find yourself needing to show your taxi driver the addresses in this guide, so we've included them in Japanese on each page

30 EXPERIENCES

1. Drink the ultimate cocktail
2. A teahouse amidst the flowers
3. Tokyo's best concept store
4. A hidden restaurant in Shibuya
5. Spend a night on a library bookshelf
6. François Simon's favorite sushi place
7. Tokyo's best onsen
8. The Michelin-starred chef who does things like no one else
9. One thousand two hundred and thirty-three shades of paper
10. Have lunch in a Japanese garden
11. The world's biggest bookstore
12. The world's smallest bookstore
13. Magic, pure and simple
14. Celebrate your "un-birthday"
15. Tokyo street-food market
16. Have dinner at the old folks'
17. Go on a bike ride in Tokyo
18. Drink yuzu juice at the Nezu Museum
19. Mini-street, maxi-bender
20. Eat peasant food
21. Organic - and then some
22. Spend a night in old Tokyo
23. Go for standing sushi
24. Treat yourself to a head spa
25. "Apply" to a restaurant
26. Have a cocktail at 771 feet altitude
27. Eat art
28. Spend a magical night outside of town
29. Stay at a capsule hotel
30. The craziest museum
...
31. Top-secret address

DRINK THE
ULTIMATE COCKTAIL

When you sip a cocktail at Gen Yamamoto, you'll feel like it's the first time you've ever had a real one.

Sit in monastic silence on one of only eight seats at this tiny bar and witness a unique mixology ceremony: a subtle procession of meticulous gestures, during which Yamamoto slices a yuzu with religious devotion, disrobes a tomato, and metes out gin and sake with the precision of a mad scientist.

Mandarin, milk vodka, and Japanese beans. Kiwi and Normandy gin. Passion fruit and whisky. In the form of six cocktails, you'll discover stunning combinations in a glass, as unexpected as they are memorable.

PHOTO CREDIT: CITYFOODSTERS

GEN YAMAMOTO
1-6-4 AZABU-JUBAN, MINATO-KU,
TOKYO, ANNIVERSARY BUILDING 1F

東京都港区麻布十番1-6-4
アニバーサリービル1F

DAILY: 3pm / 11pm (EXCEPT MON)	Reservation by e-mail required office@genyamamoto.jp www.genyamamoto.jp +81 3-6434-0652	4 cocktails: 5,500 yen 6 cocktails: 7,500 yen

#02

A TEA HOUSE
AMIDST THE FLOWERS

At first glance, it looks like a nice little neighborhood flower shop. But hidden away behind the bouquets, in a greenhouse overflowing with flowers, you'll find a teahouse that's pure zen. Waitresses wearing cloth florist's aprons dispense teapots brimming with herbal brews made from herbs cut fresh that morning. Stop here to catch your breath before or after a hectic run around town.

AOYAMA FLOWER MARKET TEA HOUSE
5-1-2 MINAMI-AOYAMA, MINATO-KU, TOKYO

東京都港区南青山5-1-2

MON - SAT: 11am / 8pm
SUN: 11am / 7pm

Reservation recommended
+81 3-3400-0887

www.afm-teahouse.com/aoyama

AOYAMA FLOWER MARKET TEA HOUSE

TOKYO'S BEST
CONCEPT STORE

If you like the Parisian concept store Merci, you'll love Japanese creator Mina Perhonen's shop. She does things like no one else.

Call (a contraction of "creation" and "all"), which opened a year ago in the Omotesando district, feels like a cheerful house where three generations work side-by-side: the youngest saleswoman is 20 years old, the oldest 83. Minä likes mixing generations in all her spaces and often hires retirees who aren't ready to stop working. At Call, as you stroll from room to room, you'll discover a grocery story, a restaurant with a patio on stilts, and a textile workshop.

PHOTO CREDIT: MASAHIRO SANBE

CALL (Enter through the Spiral store, then take the elevator on the left to 5th floor) **5-6-23 MINAMI-AOYAMA, MINATO-KU, TOKYO, SPIRAL, 5th FLOOR**	東京都港区南青山5-6-23 SPIRAL5階	
MON - SUN: 11am / 8pm	+81 3-6825-3733	www.mp-call.jp

A HIDDEN RESTAURANT
IN SHIBUYA

They say that hopeless romantics fall in love three times a day. In Yuri Nomura's case, it happens with every meal. Her greatest love affair is with food. After studying in England and cutting her culinary teeth in the kitchens of Paris and San Francisco (at Alice Waters' famous flagship, Chez Panisse), she came back to Japan and opened Eatrip, a small oasis of green, hidden away in the chaos of Shibuya.

Under a skylight, on large wooden tables, she serves up simple dishes, colorful and suffused with sweetness, made from local, seasonal, and organic ingredients. Her inspiration? The food of her childhood, which conjures up memories and feelings. Don't even think about coming to Tokyo without stopping to eat here.

EATRIP
6-31-10 JINGUMAE
SHIBUYA-KU TOKYO, 1F

東京都渋谷区神宮前6-31-10

DINNER: TUE - SAT: 6pm / midnight
SAT: 11:30am / 3pm
SUN: 11:30am / 5pm

Reservation required
+81 3-3409-4002
shibuya@mail.com

www.restaurant-eatrip.com

INTERVIEW

- **YURI NOMURA** -
CHEF OF EMOTIONS

Fascinated by the connection between what we feel and what we eat, Yuri is setting out to create a "laboratory of emotions". An irresistible encounter.

What were you like as a child?

I was a real foodie. My mother ran a cooking school, so I've always been surrounded by people who loved to eat. And while it's true that I've always been interested in cooking, I never thought I'd make it my profession. I saw cooking as a "girlie thing". And I preferred "boys' talk"! Then I went to study in England and when I came back, I found myself wanting to start cooking.

What are your influences?

First of all, sharing: when you work side-by-side, you create a community, and that's what gives us strength. For me, cooking is the best way to meet people I love, who love the same things as I do. And, finally, home cooking.

What does cooking mean to you?

It means cooking from the heart – it doesn't need to be anything elaborate. This is going to be a place for culinary performances that evoke emotions and memories through the flavors of the dishes.

What's your favorite childhood dish?

A mimosa cake my mother used to make for guests. She always kept some in the fridge for the many visitors who stopped by. And over the course of the day, I would sneak a little piece here, a little piece there...

What's the typical childhood dish in Japan?

Miso soup!

> *I'm going to open a laboratory of emotions soon*

SPEND A NIGHT ON
A LIBRARY BOOKSHELF

Nothing beats falling asleep while doing what you love most in the world. For the architects Makoto Tanijiri and Ai Yoshida, that means reading. On the 8th floor of an office building, they've created a library with tiny encapsulated rooms where you can spend the night or simply doze off for an afternoon nap.

Just choose a book – a manga or a travel or adventure novel in English or Japanese – slip into your bunk, and pull the curtain shut.

PHOTO CREDIT: @AG.LR.88

BOOK AND BED TOKYO
1-17-7, NISHI IKEBUKURO, TOSHIMA-KU, TOKYO, LUMIERE BUILLDING 7F

東京都豊島区西池袋1-17-7 ルミエールビル7階

DAILY: check-in 4pm / 11pm check-out 11am DURING THE DAY*: 1pm / 5pm	Prices start at 5,000 yen for the night Day stays are 500 yen per hour	bookandbedtokyo.com/en/tokyo/index.html

* beds are not available during the day

BOOK AND BED TOKYO

FRANÇOIS SIMON'S
FAVORITE SUSHI PLACE

We would never have heard of this sushi place if it weren't for the great French food critic, François Simon (the inspiration behind Anton Ego in the animated film, *Ratatouille*), who manages to unearth hidden gastronomic gems around the world. He dug this particular one up in the district of Omotesando, on the ground floor of an office building.

Makoto, the owner, has been expertly wielding a knife for 50 years: he rolled sushi in restaurants all over Tokyo before opening this discreetly charming spot with its cheerful team. Enter and ask for omakase, which means "I'll leave it up to you," and give the sushi master carte blanche. Then watch as a parade of sushi, sashimi, and grilled fish (sardines, sole, octopus, shrimp, tuna…) appears before your eyes – a total of 12 to 15 pieces of incomparable goodness and delicacy.

KIDOGUCHI SUSHI
5-6-3 MINAMIAOYAMA
MINATO TOKYO, B1F

東京都港区南青山5-6-3 メゾンブランシュ半地下

| Open daily, but Sunday and Monday openings are irregular, so call in advance | +81 3-5467-3992 Reservation required | Lunch 3,000 yen Dinner 20,000 yen |

- FRANÇOIS SIMON -
FOOD CRITIC

François Simon is the undercover food critic of Paris. Everyone knows him, but no one has ever seen him; he tests restaurants surreptitiously. An incurable Nipponophile who has traveled to Japan repeatedly, he knows Tokyo like the back of his hand.

What fascinates you about Japan?

Japan has taught me how to be innocent again. I've been coming here for 25 years, and I realized that I was starting to form a much too precise opinion of this country. I was basically waiting for people to ask me, "Hey, what do you think about Japan?" Because I had an answer for everything.

And then I realized that I actually don't know anything anymore. I've forgotten everything and find myself approaching things like a child again, with just my eyes and memories, without my intellect butting in and imposing structure on it all.

The easier things are, the less I know and that makes me feel comfortable

Japan tastes like a grain of rice

What's the flavor of Japan?

What's interesting about a grain of rice is isolating the soft heart from the shell when you bite into it.

Last time you came to Japan, you went...

... to Sapporo. I was originally supposed to try out a fancy restaurant, but I told my buddy that I wanted to get to know the real Sapporo. So he took me to a bohemian restaurant, a sort of merry student mess, a bit dusty, where we drank sake and chewed the fat in every language. For me, that's how you get to "the heart of a grain of rice".

What approach to traveling do you recommend?

There are two mountains you should try to cross – those of prejudice and comfort. Because, on the other side of those mountains, you'll discover an amazing reward waiting for you: you'll find there's everything to discover. For example, going for onigiri at 7-Eleven at two o'clock in the morning, taking small, slow provincial trains rather than the Shinkansen bullet train, picking up a bento box at the station and eating it on the train while watching the landscape roll by, staying in youth hostels, going to unfamiliar neighborhoods, to museums no one else goes to... In short, making yourself do things that are outside your comfort zone but that teach you something new.

You feel very small, so you keep your mouth shut and taste in Japan, in silence

Get away from what you are and let Japan pervade you

TOKYO'S
BEST ONSEN

This onsen is enormous and its typically ancient-Tokyo décor is inspired by the traditional Edo period. You walk around wrapped in a yukata, a summer kimono, which they lend you at the entrance. We recommend beginning with a stroll amidst the maple trees in the Japanese gardens and a foot bath in the creek before disrobing and sinking into the hot baths, first inside, then outside.

Finally, top it all off with a nap, ensconced in one of the onsen's massage armchairs. By the time you leave, you'll feel like you're walking on clouds.

CROSS TOKYO BAY
ON THE ELEVATED TRAIN

To get to this onsen, which is pretty far from central Tokyo, take advantage of the opportunity to ride the Yurikamome elevated train (the name means "black-headed gull", a bird that lives in Tokyo Bay). Just over 9 miles long, the line crosses the sea over the Rainbow Bridge. Prepare to be amazed. Get off at the Telecom Center station.

OEDO ONSEN MONOGATARI
2-6-3 AOMI, KOTO-KU
TOKYO

東京都江東区青海2-6-3

DAILY: 11am / 9am
open all night

+81 3-5500-1126

daiba.ooedoonsen.jp/en/

ONSEN
USER'S GUIDE

Hot baths are a Japanese obsession. Before or after the evening meal, to "clean the soul", Japanese families head to an onsen (open-air hot spring) or sento (neighborhood public bath). There are baths for women and baths for men. Everyone carries their own bath bucket and a rolled towel on their forehead to protect their hair and keep their head cool.

Get undressed:

wearing a bathing suit is prohibited

(as is having a tattoo)

Your only accessory:

a micro-towel for your head

Head to the showers

Grab a bath bucket

Take a seat on a little bench

and wash yourself thoroughly

Sink into the bath

Caution: the water is very hot – around 107°F, sometimes more

THE MICHELIN-STARRED CHEF
WHO DOES THINGS LIKE NO ONE ELSE

Den is the only Michelin-starred chef with a sense of humor. If you ask his fellow star-winning colleague Alain Passard of L'Arpège in Paris for his favorite restaurant in Tokyo, he'll immediately slip you this address under the table. Den's restaurant is considered one of the 50 best in the world. Each of his dishes features some incredible sleight of hand that invariably makes his customers laugh. An emoji carved into a carrot, an ant hidden in a salad on purpose... A sense of humor this great requires great seriousness. His obsession: to reboot young people's idea of traditional Japanese cuisine. And it's working.

PHOTO CREDIT: PAOLO STA. BARBARA

JIMBOCHO DEN
2-3-18 JINGUMAE, SHIBUYA-KU, TOKYO,
ARCHITECT HOUSE HALL JIA

東京都渋谷区神宮前2-3-18 建築家会館JIA館

LUNCH: hours vary DINNER: 6pm / 11pm SUN: closed	+81 3-6455-5433 Reservation required	www.jimbochoden.com

- DEN -

MICHELIN-STARRED CHEF

Where did you pick up this surprising way of cooking?

From my mother, who was a geisha. She taught me how to cook, but above all the art of entertaining your customers. I never went to cooking school, but I did my first apprenticeship in her ryotei (a restaurant run by geishas). The customers, who were in cahoots with her, would constantly send my dishes back to the kitchen to teach me humility. It made me understand that I shouldn't think about myself when I cook, but about my customers. Because if I think about them first, they'll do the same for me.

My mother was a geisha

What kinds of dishes do you cook?

I don't know how to cook anything but traditional Japanese cuisine. Yet I've noticed that young people tend not to eat it anymore; there are too many rules. I thought that was a shame, so I decided to make it fashionable again by making it fun, by getting rid of the taboos.

For me, cooking should be a language, a memory I share with my customers, whom I don't consider customers so much as friends. When they're in my restaurant, I want them to feel like they're in my home. As it happens, I often personalize my dishes with a drawing, image, or name – something I know about my customer.

How do you come up with your dishes?

We talk about things a lot as a team and compose dishes together, based on our mood at the time. For example, since it isn't customary to have coffee after dessert in Japan, I appropriated a Starbucks mug to make a dessert with a totally unexpected cappuccino-truffle flavor. Since I lost a Michelin star last year, I wrote Starbacks in the hope of winning back a star! Every dish is a story. As far as the ant in the salad is concerned, I put it there on purpose since it's reminiscent of the food our Japanese ancestors ate.

What's the best advice you've ever been given?

The only constant in life is change. That's advice from my mother – I think about it every time I cook. She's 59 years old now. And she's still a geisha!

PHOTO CREDIT: CITY FOODSTERS

1233 SHADES
OF PAPER

Founded in 1904, this is a 10-story temple to paper: over 1,000 different colors, available as paper, envelopes, origami paper, notebooks, greeting cards, giftwrap (the famous Japanese washi), postcards, and 1,200 types of pens of all dimensions and tip sizes. Incidentally, the colors here aren't numbered but have unusual names instead: sheep skin, little mermaid...

Artists, writers, and designers all flock here for supplies. As for us, we left with 17 pens, almost 7 pounds of paper, and 5 notebooks to fill.

Our two favorite floors:
The 2nd, "Letters", which is dedicated to snail mail and even has stamps and a mailbox.
The 10th, "Farm", where you'll find a vegetable garden with incredibly fresh lettuce, which will go on to be harvested and served in the restaurant directly upstairs.

ITOYA
2-7-15 GINZA, CHUO-KU
TOKYO

東京都中央区銀座2-7-15

DAILY: 10am / 8pm | +81 3-3561-8311 | www.ito-ya.co.jp

HAVE LUNCH IN
A JAPANESE GARDEN

If you're crazy about tofu, come satisfy your tofu cravings at Tofuya Ukai, a traditional house with Japanese gardens inspired by the Edo period. Here even the waitresses wear hakama, the "working girl's kimono", with pleated pants that make it easier for them to walk.

The tofu, which is prepared in-house, is offered up in all its forms: age-dengaku (fried over charcoal and basted with sweet-savory miso sauce), tosui-tofu (mixed with soymilk and served in a ceramic bowl), and yuba (tofu skin, a Kyoto specialty).

Take a seat on the tatamis looking out onto the magnificent Japanese gardens, watch the sliding doors close, and let the long procession of dishes begin.

 TOFUYA UKAI
4-4-13 SHIBA-KOEN, MINATO-KU, TOKYO

東京都港区芝公園4-4-13

| DAILY: 11am / 10pm closed once a month call in advance as day varies | +81 3-3436-1028 Reservation required | www.ukai.co.jp/english/shiba/ |

WHAT IS THE EDO PERIOD?

The Edo was a key period in the cultural construction of Japan because it was the era (between 1603 and 1868) during which the country closed itself off to foreign influences and developed its local culture. As a result, most of the artisanal crafts associated with traditional Japanese culture today have their roots in the Edo period.

THE WORLD'S
BIGGEST BOOKSTORE

A 180-foot-long "magazine street" that runs across three gigantic buildings. The Tsutaya Daikanyama bookstore, considered one of the 20 most beautiful bookstores in the world, is a magazine lover's temple, a six-floor modern maze of everything that exists in terms of reading material, both Japanese and international: literature, cooking, travel, cars, art, architecture, music... And it's open until 2am. Pretty mind-blowing.

TIP: Don't forget to go up to the 1st floor of the main building, where you'll find the bookshop Anjin. You can lounge on enormous sofas and have a drink while browsing one of the 30,000 vintage magazines rounded up from antique shops around the world.

TSUTAYA
16-15 SARUGAKUCHO,
SHIBUYA-KU, TOKYO

東京都渋谷区猿楽町16-15

| DAILY: 7am / 2pm | +81 3-3770-2525 | real.tsite.jp/daikanyama/english/index.html |

THE WORLD'S
SMALLEST BOOKSTORE

A single room with a single book: that's the rule for this micro-bookstore, which is a perfect example of Japanese-style minimalism. A new book is chosen every week – a new universe, really, since the entire room is tailored to the featured book. You can buy the book, but also meet its author and see objects associated with it.

PHOTO CREDIT: MIYUKI KANEKO COURTESY TAKRAM

 MORIOKA SHOTEN & CO
1-28-15 GINZA, CHUO-KU, TOKYO,
1F SUZUKI BUILDING

東京都中央区銀座
1-28-15 鈴木ビル 1F

DAILY: 1pm / 8pm
(EXCEPT MON)

+81 3-3535-5020

MAGIC,
PURE AND SIMPLE

In an alley in the Ginza district, a door opens onto a small, completely black room with a large table and eight chairs. You enter and sit down. Silence. First, mysterious sounds, then a bamboo forest appears on the walls, flowers begin to grow, butterflies flutter. A shower of petals rains down on your table, which turns into a river as a butterfly takes off from your plate.

You're at Tokyo's MoonFlower Sagaya Ginza, Art by teamLab . There aren't many such digital restaurants in the world, and this is the most accessible. It's expensive, yes, but so incredibly beautiful, magical, and delicious that it's worth traveling across the entire world just to come here.

PHOTO CREDIT: MOONFLOWER SAGAYA GINZA, TOKYO, JAPAN © TEAMLAB

MOONFLOWER SAGAYA GINZA, ART BY TEAMLAB
2-5-19 GINZA, CHUO-KU, TOKYO, 6F, PUZZLE GINZA

東京都中央区銀座 2-5-19
PUZZLE 銀座 6F

DAILY: at 7pm

+81 3-6263-2525
Reservation required

moonflower-sagaya.com

MOONFLOWER SAGAYA GINZA,
ART BY TEAMLAB

CELEBRATE YOUR "UN-BIRTHDAY"

On a busy street in the Shibuya district, two restaurants face each other. In one of them, the customers are all men; in the other, all women. In the men's restaurant, you eat fish in peace and quiet; in the women's, skewers are served amidst singing. Two types of food, two different atmospheres that taunt each other, each trying to outdo the other in the number of customers they can pull in from the street. We chose our team – the women's, which holds the trump card: celebrating birthdays like you've never seen before.

TIP: Call ahead, tell them it's the birthday of one of your fellow diners… We won't tell you what happens next.

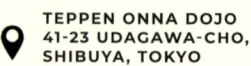

TEPPEN ONNA DOJO
41-23 UDAGAWA-CHO,
SHIBUYA, TOKYO

東京都渋谷区宇田川町
41-23　第二大久保ビル1F

DAILY: 5pm / midnight   +81 3-5428-3698
Reservation recommended

Prices start at 2,000 yen

TOKYO
STREET-FOOD MARKET

An artisanal beer brewery, a Brooklyn-style burger truck, a vegan stand, a shack serving fish cooked with a blowtorch, a tapas trailer… Enough said – yep, welcome to hipsterville. Commune 2nd, at the heart of Omotesando, is an eclectic and colorful street-food market where you choose what you want to drink and eat and then sit down together at big wooden tables. On some evenings there are open-air concerts. Quintessential Japanese hipsterdom.

COMMUNE 2ND
3-13 MINAMI-AOYAMA,
MINATO-KU, TOKYO

東京都港区南青山3-13

DAILY: 11am / 10pm

commune2nd.com

STREET MARKET COMMUNE 2ND

"JAPANESEISMS"

There are certain words that exist only in Japanese because you can only perceive the state of being, mood, or feeling they describe through the lens of Japanese culture. Here, we've selected our six favorite "Japaneseisms" for you.

Komorebi

木漏れ日

*SUN RAYS

Sunlight filtering through the leaves of a tree.

Shinrinyoku

森林浴

*FOREST BATH

Taking a forest bath means going for a walk deep in the woods where there's nothing but silence, peace and relaxation.

Yuugen

---

*THE BEAUTY OF A PLACE

Perceiving the universe in a way that unleashes emotions
that are too deep and mysterious to express in words..

Shoganai

---

*THE VICISSITUDES OF LIFE

"There's nothing you can do, that's just how it is". Accepting that something is
out of your control in any event and that you need to keep going without regret.

Hijiame

肘雨

*ELBOW RAIN

In Japan, there are 50 different expressions for rain, but our favorite is elbow rain: a shower so sudden that you don't even have time to get out your umbrella and have to cover yourself with your elbows.

Wabisabi

わびさび

*BEAUTY OF TIME PASSING

It's imperfect, ephemeral, worn with age? That's precisely what makes it beautiful. This esthetic of time passing is known as wabisabi.

 SOSAIBOU
4-1-9 MEGURO-HONCHO,
MEGURO-KU, TOKYO

東京都目黒区目黒本町4-1-9

MON - FRI: 6pm / midnight Closed on the weekends and holidays	+81 3-3710-4336 Reservation required	Menu starting at 7,000 yen

HAVE DINNER
AT THE OLD FOLKS'

What is this anyway? Their living room? Kitchen? Restaurant? One thing is for sure: Katsuro and Mieko are the owners of Sosaibou. He's the poet, serving up dishes that seem like they've been conjured up by magic; she's the party animal, pouring the sake. They must be at least 80 years old and can't live without each other: two diminutive eccentrics who've been serving "zen" cuisine, inspired by monks, for 33 years.

Their dishes combine every possible color, shape, and flavor. For Katsuro, it's a metaphor for the medley of life: some things are bitter, some sweet – and you simply have to accept it.

A place of joy, wisdom, and... inebriation.

WHAT IS ZEN CUISINE?

In Japan, it's called shojin ryori: the cuisine of the monks, an 800-year-old philosophy inspired by the seasons and prepared without meat or fish... and without onions, leeks, garlic, or other root vegetables, since harvesting them means killing them.

TOKYO, 5AM IN THE MORNING

#17

GO ON A
BIKE RIDE IN TOKYO

Yanaka is Tokyo's oldest neighborhood, one of the rare areas that has preserved its temples, wood houses, and peaceful alleyways, which resound with the gentle clattering of bicycles... Speaking of: do like the locals and go for a ride around Yanaka on a bike, which you can rent from tokyobike. This design boutique, which doubles as a coffee and lifestyle shop, is dedicated to bicycle lovers, of which there are many in Japan – devotees who take their bikes with them everywhere: on the subway and to the office, even going so far as to sleep with them. As you can see from the hipster Instagram account @tokyobike_jp, which is dedicated entirely to these pedal-powered two-wheelers.

TOKYOBIKE
4-2-39 YANAKA, TAITŌ, TOKYO

東京都台東区谷中4-2-39

DAILY: 10am / 7:30pm   +81 3-5809-0980   tokyobikerentals.com

TOKYOBIKE

FIVE THINGS TO DO
BY BIKE IN YANAKA

- meditate in the zen gardens of the Nezu-jinja Shrine, a traditional Shinto sanctuary

- visit SCAI THE BATHHOUSE, a contemporary art gallery located in a former onsen

- discover the underside of umbrellas and other design objects at the KONCENT boutique in Kuramae

- taste and buy tea at Nakamura Tea Life Store, a traditional teahouse

- create your own personalized planner or ideal color of ink at the stationery store Kakimori

DRINK YUZU JUICE
AT THE NEZU MUSEUM

It's the little pleasures that add spice to the day. For example: stealing off to the Nezu Museum in Minato, slipping past the bamboo screen, following the pebble pathway, buying your ticket to this museum dedicated to traditional Japanese arts and crafts, passing through the exhibition rooms, opening the door to the Nezu Café, taking a seat at a table overlooking the lush Japanese gardens, ordering a glass of yuzu juice, pressing your face against the window and... simply savoring the moment.

PHOTO CREDIT: FUJITSUKA MITSUMASA

 NEZU MUSEUM
6-5-1 MINAMI-AOYAMA,
MINATO-KU, TOKYO

東京都港区南青山6-5-1

DAILY: 10am / 5pm
(EXCEPT MON)

+81 3-3400-2536

You must purchade a ticket
to the Nezu Museum
to enter the café

NEZU MUSEUM GARDEN

19

MINI-STREET
MAXI-BENDER

No, not that one – the other one. Because, yes, you'll definitely hear everyone talking about the famous Golden Gai, the working-class neighborhood teeming with bars that's more commonly known as the "neighborhood of thirst". As for us, what we're talking about is "drunkards' lane", right behind the train tracks of Shibuya, which you'll find thanks to the rows of lanterns hanging over the entrance. Behind them lies an alleyway full of tiny bars that serve sake. Our favorite: the one at the end of the street, spattered with graffiti, which you access via a miniscule staircase. It only has room for four customers, but also offers karaoke. Just ask the boss – he likes to sing too. Prepare to leave lurching, but in very high spirits.

 **SHIBUYA NONBEI YOKOCHO
1-25 SHIBUYA, SHIBUYA-KU,
TOKYO**

東京都渋谷区渋谷一丁目25

Go here after dinner

EAT
PEASANT FOOD

Robata means "fireside cooking" and that's exactly what awaits you when you walk into Robata Honten. This intimate restaurant has many stories to tell, with its 100-year-old façade, walls overflowing with books, drapes, and dishes, and period furniture that's even older than its 74-year-old owner. His name is Inoue Takao: he's a Japanese film and literature buff, and has followed in his father's and grandfather's footsteps, preparing food in the peasant tradition, served on enormous dishes for sharing. Juliette Binoche and Catherine Deneuve have made this their go-to place in Tokyo.

ROBATA HONTEN
1-3-8 YURAKUCHO,
CHIYODA-KU, TOKYO

東京都 千代田区有楽町1-3-8

DAILY: 5pm / 11pm
(EXCEPT SUN)

+81 3-3591-1905
Reservation recommended

Prices start at 5,000 yen
per person

ROBATA HONTEN

ORGANIC
AND THEN SOME

Biotop is the Dover Street Market of organic products: a concept store based around plants and flowers that's focused on the environment and reinvests 1% of its profits in reforestation projects in Japan. What's remarkable about this boutique, created by the Japanese brand Adam et Ropé, is its atypical and inspiring architecture.

This is the meeting spot for designers and creatives, and the place where all influential (and eco-friendly) brands are launched. Don't miss the bar–restaurant Irving Place, made entirely of wood, on the fourth floor, or the tree house, a little shack in a tree that you can climb, overlooking the courtyard.

At Biotop, bio and organic products gets top priority.

BIOTOP
4-6-44 SHIROKANEDAI,
MINATO-KU, TOKYO

東京都港区白金台4-6-44

DAILY: 11am / 8pm +81 3-3444-2421 www.biotop.jp

SPEND A NIGHT
IN OLD TOKYO

… and wake up on a tatami mat. Greet your neighbors and ride a bike through the district's small alleyways. Hanare – a guest house-cum-hotel-cum-traditional inn located in the peaceful Yanaka district – offers total immersion in the local life.

A stay at Hanare is basically a stay in the neighborhood: you get to experience the same places as the locals. So you might wake up in a room at one end of the street and grab breakfast at the other, before going to the sento (public baths) on another street. In the evening, slip on geta (those famous Japanese wooden flip-flop clogs), enter your completely empty room, and unroll your futon and duvet on the tatami mats. Lights out: good night!

HANARE
HAGISO, 3-10-25 YANAKA,
TAITO-KU, TOKYO

東京都台東区谷中3-10-25
HAGISO

CHECK IN: 3pm / 9pm
CHECK OUT: 11am

+81 3-5834-7301
www.hanare.hagiso.jp/en

About 20,000 yen
for a room

 UOGASHI NIHON-ICHI
25-6 UDAGAWACHO,
SHIBUYA-KU, TOKYO

MON - FRI: 10am / 22:30pm
(last admission)

+81 3-5728-5451

東京都渋谷区宇田川町25-6

www.uogashi-nihonichi.
com/english/

GO FOR **STANDING SUSHI**

The line stretches all the way out onto the street, but it's definitely worth the wait. Hundreds of hungry bellies parade through this typical Shibuya standing sushi bar to indulge in the fleeting pleasure of eating top-notch sushi while standing at the counter: fatty tuna, scallops, sea urchins. Three chefs prepare delicacies non-stop every minute through midnight. Ten little pieces of sushi later and you're ready to roll again.

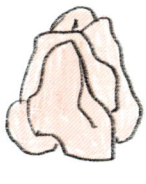

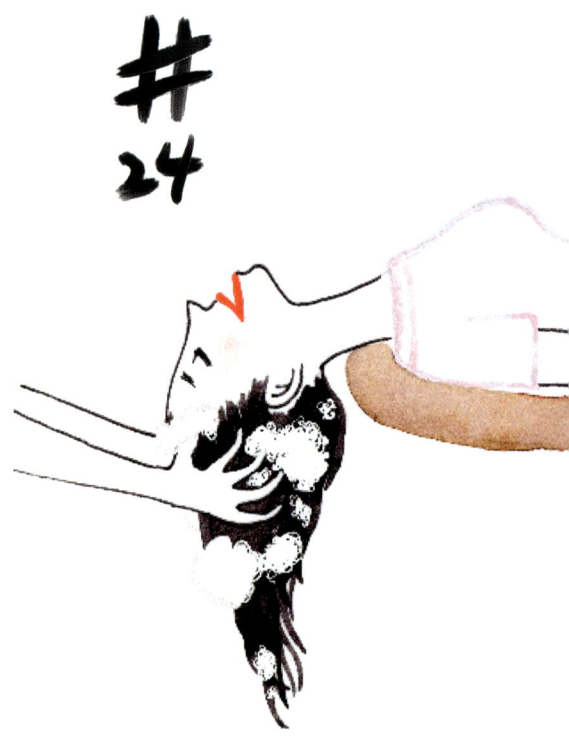

TREAT YOURSELF
TO A HEAD SPA
3 BEAUTY SALONS

Head massages are a ritual the Japanese indulge in regularly to unwind after a long day. Where? At head spas, which specialize in hair and head care. We've picked out three for you, to ensure that you get a head massage that's truly out of this world.

> THE MOST HEAVENLY:

It's ridiculous – literally, since this bohemian hair salon located in a small apartment is actually called Ridicule, French for ridiculous. The house specialty: the head spa, a divinely delicious head massage.

RIDICULE
3-31-13 JINGUMAE,
SHIBUYA-KU, TOKYO

東京都渋谷区神宮前3-31-13

| MON - SAT: 11am / 9pm
SUN: 11am / 7pm
HOLIDAYS: 11am / 7pm | +81 3-3478-7332
Reservation required | www.ridicule.jp |

> THE MOST TRANSCENDENTAL:

It's a bit far to get to (45 minutes from downtown Tokyo), but it's absolutely worth it. At this hair spa, they'll wash, massage, and do your hair while you lie cradled in a cocoon-like hammock.

COCONA
3-16-1 KOENJI-KITA, SUGINAMI-KU, 2F,3F

東京都杉並区高円寺北3-16-1
田中ビル2.3階

DAILY: 9:30am / 9pm
(EXCEPT TUE)

+81 3-5356-6543
Reservation required

salon-cocona.com

> THE MOST TARGETED:

At Uka, they start by giving you a detailed hair-and-scalp diagnosis before bringing you to a private room to minister exclusively to you. Depending on the time of day, you can choose shampoo with chamomile, lavender, and rosemary extracts to put you to sleep ("Nighty night!") or with peppermint for an energizing boost ("Wake up!"). Then they wash your hair, massaging the pressure points on your scalp and at the base of your neck with alternatingly firm and gentle gestures. Finally, they wrap up your hair in a heated towel before styling or blow-drying it. You'll emerge 45 minutes later, feeling relaxed from toe to head.

UKA TOKYO MIDTOWN,
9-7-4 AKASAKA, MINATOKU,
TOKYO GALLERIA 2F

東京都港区赤坂9-7-4 東京ミッドタウン ガレリア2F

MON - SAT: 10am / 11pm
SUN : 10am / 10pm

+81 3-5413-7236
Reservation required

www.uka.co.jp/salons/midtown/

COCONA HAIRDRESSER

"APPLY" TO **A RESTAURANT**

This is a restaurant you have to earn: to eat at Bohemian, you must send a "cover letter" or know someone who knows someone who knows someone... It makes sense, though: there are only two tables in the entire place, and Kazu, the chef, is a gastronomic visionary. He's already been to Burning Man and is obsessed with cooking in the craziest places in the world.

Seasonal fish, bell peppers, corn, shellfish, mushrooms, brochettes... Kazu prepares everything over a fire, according to the traditional method used by the fishermen of Hokkaido, who used to cook on their boats. So take a seat at the irori, the traditional table with an opening in the middle for the fire, massaging your bare feet on little round pellets, and let the ceremony begin.

Listen, we'll even give you a little leg up... Here's where you should send your cover letter: kazu@playearth.jp

 **BOHEMIAN SECRET**

Send an application email to: kazu@playearth.jp

HAVE A COCKTAIL
AT 771 FEET ALTITUDE

The Park Hyatt Shinjuku Hotel is where the iconic scenes from the movie Lost in Translation were shot. Take the elevator up to the New York Bar on the 53rd floor starting at 5pm to snag one of the two best seats: either Bill Murray alias Bob Harris's spot at the bar, or the one with the dizzying view to the left of the bar.

There's a jazz concert every night. Order the "L.I.T." – as in Lost in Translation – cocktail (sake, peach, cranberry, and cherry liqueur), or "Sugar Blues" (Rittenhouse Rye, yuzu, Coke, Amer Picon, egg white, and lemon juice). And lose yourself... in the "translations."

Live Jazz starting from 8pm from Monday to Saturday and from 7pm on Sunday.

 PARK HYATT
3-7-1-2 NISHI SHINJUKU, SHINJUKU-KU, TOKYO

東京都東京都新宿区西新宿 3-7-1-2

| MON - WED: 8pm / 11:45pm
THU - SAT: 8pm / 12:30am
SUN: 7pm / 10:45pm | +81 3-5322-1234
Reservation recommended | tokyo.park.hyatt.com |

"RENÉ MAGRITTE DINNER FOR DELVAUX" 2015
PHOTO CREDIT: MASAYUKI SAITO

#27

EAT
ART

You don't know the address or who you'll be with. In fact, up until the last minute, you have no idea what's about to happen. All you do know is that it's going to be a truly memorable night. The mysterious Ayako Suwa is a performance artist who organizes guerilla restaurants in Tokyo at which guests are party to extraordinary culinary experiences. Like nothing you've ever eaten before.

But – we're leaving it up to you to figure out how to get yourself put on the list of potential guests.

 FOOD CREATION

Find out about upcoming events at **www.foodcreation.jp/en/**

"TASTE OF PHOTOGRAPHY" 2015
PHOTO CREDIT: NAOHIRO UDAGAWA

"TASTE OF LUNASOL" 2015
PHOTO CREDIT: LUNASOL

PHOTO CREDIT: ITTETSU MATSUOKA

- AYAKO SUWA -
CULINARY ARTIST

The artist Ayako Suwa has worked for Dior, Agnès B, contemporary museums, and big-name chefs. Her obsession: retranscribing the taste of emotions into flavors. She has created the taste of anxiety blended slowly with that of terror, guilt, pride, melancholy... Ayako turns cooking into a profound life experience.

When was this desire of yours for a guerilla restaurant born?

When I was four years old. I grew up in nature, which simultaneously terrified and attracted me. Jellyfish in the sea, insects in flowers – everything fascinated me. So I decided to organize a guerilla restaurant: I prepared a tea party with dead insects, pollen, and flowers, and invited kids who were younger than me and ate it all without knowing what it was.

We eat to live, taste to grow

What fuels your inspiration?

Desire, curiosity, and the urge to eat. When I see people on the street, I like to ask myself what they eat, how they live, and so on.

What's your most recent discovery?

It was in the sea: some strangely shaped seaweed I'd never seen before. In fact, what I look for in food isn't a good taste but the element of surprise.

How does a guerilla restaurant work?

From the moment guests arrive, they're plunged into a special universe. Starting from when they sit down at the table, they have to respect certain rules. Namely, they must:
- keep their eyes closed;
- eat with their hands;
- consume each offering in a single mouthful; and
- do so at the same time as the other guests. To share in the same sensation.

How do you conceive of your guerilla restaurants upstream?

I think of them as a bit like ceremonies. My waiters are artists to whom I assign roles, characters even. The question I ask myself each time is: How can I best express the taste of this experience? How can I make a deep impression on my guests to ensure they leave with lasting memories?

I only like to eat bizarre things

"JOURNEY ON THE TABLE WITH VVG TAIPEI" 2012
PHOTO CREDIT: VVG

📍 **HOSHINOYA KARUIZAWA, KITASAKU-GUN, NAGANO, 389-0194**

長野県北佐久郡軽井沢町長倉 2148

For exceptional occasions only since it's very expensive prices start at 52,000 yen / night

+81 50-3786-1144
Reservation required

hoshinoya.com/karuizawa/en/

SPEND A MAGICAL NIGHT **OUTSIDE OF TOWN**
3 RYOKANS OUTSIDE OF TOKYO

> A LUXURY RYOKAN

For just one night, leave the Tokyo crowds behind for this dreamlike spot straight out of a Miyazaki movie: the Hoshinoya Karuizawa resort, a large ryokan with a peaceful onsen, stone paths, and small wooden pagodas all clustered around a lake in the middle of the woods. At nightfall, a boat glides beneath your window to light the dozens of floating lanterns that shimmer in the dark like fireflies. There's a private onsen in each pagoda, but you can also climb up to the Meditation Bath, hot baths in a room with shoji screen walls.

one hour outside of Tokyo by bullet train

WHAT'S A RYOKAN?

A ryokan is a traditional Japanese inn, built using typical materials (wood, bamboo, rice paper, tatami mats) and with minimalist furnishings (low tables, sliding partitions, futons). You move them aside at the end of the day since the rooms serve as both bedrooms and living rooms. Though there aren't many ryokans in Tokyo, there are a lot more in Kyoto and in the Japanese countryside.

> A PRIVATE BATH IN THE MOUNTAINS

With its panoramic bedroom views of the sea, the Kazekomichi ryokan is located in the city of Atami with its magnificent palm trees and coastline. The best time of day to enjoy the view: in the morning, looking out from your private hot bath on the terrace as the sun rises over the sea.

30 minutes outside of Tokyo by bullet train

WATEI-KAZEKOMICHI
28-18 BAIEN-CHO, ATAMI,
SHIZUOKA

静岡県熱海市梅園町28-18

Prices start at 38,000 yen / night for two people

contact@kazekomichi.jp

kazekomichi.jp/en/

THE DISCREET CHARM OF THE SHINKANSEN

The landscapes are so beautiful in Japan that the experience of journeying by train can be just as important as the destination. To get out of Tokyo, you can take small provincial trains or, to save time, the shinkansen bullet train.
Before getting on the train at Tokyo station, choose a take-out bento box at Ekibenya Matsuri (in the station's main hall) and savor it as you watch the landscape slide by.

> JAPAN'S BEST ONSEN

Located in the city of Kusatsu, the Kusatsu Onsen was voted Japan's best, above all for the therapeutic quality of its water, but also for the beauty of its hot springs, which intersect right in the middle of the city, forming little rivers. Spend the day here and then sleep at the Boun Hotel.

about two and a half hours from Tokyo by bullet + local train

KUSATSU ONSEN BOUN
433-1 KUSATSU-MACHI,
AGATSUMA-GUN, GUNMA, JAPAN

群馬県吾妻郡草津町433-1

Prices start at 30,000 yen / night for two people

+81 279-88-3251

www.hotelboun.com

STAY AT A
CAPSULE HOTEL

Tokyo is teeming with capsule hotels, which are designed to optimize space by offering rows of stacked and side-by-side sleeping pods instead of rooms. Claustrophobics beware! Our personal favorite is the Nine Hours, where customers stay for precisely that long: enough time to sleep – and maybe even then some. It looks like an intergalactic space station and offers all the classiness and technology we love so much about Japan: sunrise alarm-clocks and ergonomic pillows; pajamas and slippers provided.

9HOURS
3F-8F 1-4-15 HYAKUNINCHO,
SHINJUKU-KU, TOKYO 169-0073

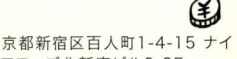

東京都新宿区百人町1-4-15 ナインアワーズ北新宿ビル3-8F

| Prices start at 5,000 yen / night | +81 3-5291-7337 | https://ninehours.co.jp/en/ |

THE CRAZIEST **MUSEUM**

We've already mentioned one of teamLab's creations, but they've struck again at the eleventh hour – and there's no way we were going to leave out their latest crazy project. This time, they've opened the Mori Building Digital Art, a truly one-of-a-kind museum where visitors will never see the same thing twice. Why? Because the works here are "alive" and react directly to contact with viewers, with the help of some 500 projectors and computers. Here, a waterfall plunges down a wall; there, you wander through a forest of lamps or along the edge of a virtual rice paddy. The goal? To show that the world has no limits. Mission accomplished.

 MORI Building DIGITAL ART MUSEUM: teamLab Borderless ODAIBA PALETTE TOWN, 1-3-8 AOMI, KOTO-KU, TOKYO, JAPAN

東京都江東区青海1-3-8 お台場パレットタウン

MON - THU: 11am / 7pm
FRI AND ON THE DAY BEFORE A HOLIDAY: 11am / 9pm
SAT: 10am / 9pm
SUN AND HOLIDAYS: 10am / 7pm

+81 3-6406-3949

Buy tickets:
https://ticket.teamlab.art

MORI BUILDING DIGITAL ART MUSEUM: TEAMLAB BORDERLESS

**We never reveal the 31st address
in the Soul of series because it's strictly confidential.
Up to you to find it!**

TOP-SECRET **ADDRESS**

The only hint we'll give you to help you find the little door to this restaurant is the address of a 7-Eleven. But here's a list of the dishes you should order once you get there: mackerel flambé; breaded corn; tuna, avocado and fish-egg bruschetta; tempura-battered king prawns; and honey tofu... Happy hunting!

Starting address:

7-ELEVEN
1-11-5 JINNAN, SHIBUYA-KU
TOKYO, 2F

東京都渋谷区神南1-11-5
ダイネス壱番館別館2F

DAILY: 5:30pm / 11:30pm

+81 3-3463-1010
Reservation required

Prices start at 4,000 yen

FOLLOW OUR ITINERARY
TO FIND THE SECRET ENTRANCE

1. Go up the stairs to the right of the 7-Eleven

2. At the top, go all the way to the end of the hallway

3. Open the old gray door on the right

4. At the very end of the hallway, there's one big door and one little door

5. Open the little door

6. Itadakimasu!*

A ROUND OF
- ☑ **SHOPPING**
- ☑ **BEAUTY**
- ☑ **KAWAII**

PASS THE BATON TO YOUR NEIGHBOR

Pass the Baton is the charming name of this modern recycling boutique, whose philosophy is to pass things you love on to their next owner. It's even more exciting to go there knowing that the pieces for sale belonged to celebrities (each label includes a photo of the A-lister, plus a little anecdote about the history of the item for sale). And to ensure that the baton truly is passed full circle, buyers can even leave a message for the previous owner.

Pass the Baton Omotesando
4-12-10 Jingumae, Shibuya-ku
Tokyo, Omotesando
Hills West Bldg B2F
4-12-10 表参道ヒルズ西館B2F東京都渋谷区神宮前4-12-10 表参道ヒルズ西館B2F
11am / 9pm Monday-Saturday
11am / 8pm Sunday and holidays
Tel: +81 3-6447-0707
www.pass-the-baton.com

LEAVIN' ON A JET PLANE...

At this boutique for travelers, you'll find travel diaries and inspiring objects that'll make you want to jump on a plane and jet off to the other side of the world pronto.

Traveler's Factory
3-13-10 Kamimeguro,
Meguro-ku,Tokyo
東京都目黒区上目黒3-13-10
or go to the branch at Narita International Airport, Terminal-1 4F
noon / 8pm, closed on Tuesdays
Tel: +81 3-6412-7830
www.travelers-factory.com

THE JAPANESE CULT BRAND

You'll sometimes feel more like you're at a contemporary art installation than in a fashion boutique at Dover Street Market, brainchild of the Japanese creator of Comme des Garçons, the cult brand that's the pride and joy of the Japanese. Here, you'll find some rare pieces from their collection, as well as a good selection by other designers. TIP: Go up to the roof – there's a surprise waiting there.

Dover Street Market
6-9-5 Ginza, Chuo-ku, Tokyo
東京都中央区銀座6-9-5
11am / 8pm
Tel: +81 3-6228-5080
ginza.doverstreetmarket.com

TOKYO'S BEST CHIC SECOND-HAND

If you're a fan of Comme des Garçons, but less so of the price tag, go to Ragtag Harajuku (a select second-hand shop) for some great deals.

Ragtag Harajuku
6-14-2 Jingumae, Shibuya-ku, Tokyo
東京都渋谷区神宮前6-14-2
11am / 8pm
Tel: +81 3-6419-3770
www.ragtag.jp

DELUXE VINTAGE

This boutique, hidden away in a residential building, is the place for all compulsive collectors of legendary Chanel pieces.

Vintage Qoo
1F, 4-11-15 Jingumae, Shibuya, Tokyo
東京都渋谷区 神宮前4-11-15 シナモンオーク1F
noon / 7pm
Tel: +81 3-6804-2017
www.qoo-online.com/

A TEMPLE TO OFF-THE-WALL FASHION

DOG Harajuku, a little boutique tucked away in a basement on an alleyway in Harajuku, is a true temple to kooky fashion. Here you'll find clothes you can't wear anywhere – unless your name happens to be Lady Gaga or Madonna... Speaking of, this is where those two style icons actually do go to pick up new outfits whenever they're in town.

DOG Harajuku
3-23-3 Jingumae Shibuya-ku Tokyo, B1 Trinity Bld.
東京都渋谷区神宮前 3-23-3、B1トリニティービル
noon / 8pm
Tel: +81 3-3746-8110
www.dog-hjk.com

RANSACK A BOUTIQUE

You'll come here to buy souvenirs for family and friends back home, and will end up picking up just as many for yourself at Tokyu Hands, the mecca of addictive gadgets of all kinds.

Tokyu Hands
12-18 Udagawacho, Shibuya-ku, Tokyo 東京都澁谷區宇田川町12-18
10am / 9pm
Tel: +81 3-5489-5111
www.tokyu-hands.co.jp

JAPANESE KNIVES

You'll find everything you need for your kitchen at Kappabashi Dori. Treat yourself to a good Japanese knife or gorgeous Japanese ceramics so you can recreate your own little tea ceremony back home.

Kappabashi-Dori
Matsugaya, 3-18-2, Taito-ku
都台東区松が谷 3-18-2
10am / 5pm

VINTAGE KIMONOS

Chicago is a cult vintage boutique in Harajuku that offers incredible deals on a selection of kimonos. Give yourself the gift of a yukata summer kimono made of light cotton, which doubles perfectly as a bathrobe.

Chicago
6-31-21 Jingumae, Shibuya-ku, Tokyo
東京都渋谷区 神宮前6-31-21 オリンピアアネックスビルB1F
11am / 8pm
Tel: +81 3-3409-5017
www.chicago.co.jp
You'll find the kimonos at the back of the boutique: they cost approx. 2,000 yen

CHOPSTICK MANIA

There are at least 1,000 pairs of chopsticks at Ginza Natsuno Aoyama: you'll even find ones for foods that are tricky to grasp (beans, tofu, etc.).

Ginza Natsuno Aoyama
4-2-17 Jingumae, Shibuya-ku, Tokyo
座夏野 青山店　東京都渋谷区神宮前 4-2-17
10am / 8pm Monday-Saturday
10am / 7pm Sunday and holidays
Tel: +81 3-3403-6033
www.e-ohashi.com

THE COFFEE SOMMELIER

The barista at this boutique dedicated to coffee lovers is a purist. Dressed in a pristine lab coat, he'll do an in-depth diagnosis of your coffee tastes before spending at least 10 minutes preparing the perfect cup for you. Definitely worth the wait.

KOFFEE MAMEYA
4-15-3 Jingumae, Shibuya-ku, Tokyo
東京都渋谷区 神宮前4-15-3
10am / 6pm

THE BEST SUPERMARKET

To jumpstart your love affair with the local food, there's nothing better than the basements of Tokyo's department stores. Our favorite is the one in Isetan, where you'll find little gems of Japanese pastries, seasonal products, caviar, Kobe beef, and sake, often prepared in-house, which you can bring back to your hotel room for a private feast on your bed or in your bathtub.

Isetan Shinjuku
Isetan food section
3-14-1, Shinjuku, Shinjuku-ku, Tokyo, B1F 東京都新宿区新宿3-14-1 B1F
10:30am / 8pm
If you want to feel what it's like to be royalty, arrive at opening time – 10:30am sharp – to experience the store's entire staff lined up and bowing 90 degrees to greet you.

NAIL SALON

The Japanese have made a virtual religion of applying gel nails, with polish that doesn't chip and stays perfectly glossy until you remove it. At least once a month, Tokyoites visit a nail salon to choose their latest nail art, with designs and colors that vary depending on the season. Uka (which we already mentioned for its exceptional head massages) is the professional home of a veritable Japanese nail virtuoso, Kiho Watanabe. At Uka, your hands will be given the same amazing treatment as your head: a massage followed by a transformation – in this case, of your nails.

Uka Tokyo Midtown
9-7-4 Galleria 2F, Akasaka, Minatoku Tokyo 東京都港区赤坂9-7-4 東京ミッドタウン ガレリア2F
10am / 9:30pm reservation required
Tel: +81 3-5413-7236
www.uka.co.jp/english/

Allow 90 minutes for a gel nail manicure and expect to pay around 10,000 yen

GET FAKE LASHES AND LOOK LIKE A REAL SHIBUYA NATIVE

Royal blue or fluorescent pink? It's your call. Choose the color, shape, and thickness of your lashes at this salon, which specializes in eyelash extensions. It takes two hours, but lasts three weeks.

Efil Lavie
5-6-5 Jingumae Shibuya-ku, Tokyo 京都渋谷区神宮前5-6-5
noon / 10pm Monday-Friday
10am / 8pm Saturday-Sunday

Closed on Tuesday
Tel: +81 3-6450-6400
Prices start at 6,400 yen for 80 lashes added.

SECRETS OF JAPANESE DRUG-STORE

You don't really know a country until you've let yourself get lost in the beauty section of a local drugstore. The stand-out chain in Tokyo is Matsumoto Kiyoshi, with its ubiquitous yellow sign. It's open until 10pm – in fact, if jetlag has you awake at all hours, the Shibuya branch is open round the clock.

Matsumoto Kyoshi
22-3, Udagawacho, Shibuya-ku, Tokyo
東京都渋谷区宇田川町22-3
open 24 hours a day
Tel: +81 3-3463-1130
www.matsukiyo.co.jp

SOME MUST-HAVE PRODUCTS:

EYE DROPS

The secret to all photo shoots: these drops, which work instantly, hydrating and soothing eyes and relieving redness. Bye-bye jet-lagged red eyes!

-> **Rohto**

ANTI-TANNING CREAM

Japanese women hate tanning and would never dream of leaving the house without sunscreen. This little sky-blue bottle offers the best value for money and has won several prizes in Japan for its texture, which blends into

the skin flawlessly, providing hydration without leaving any icky greasy residue.
-> **Biore UV 50 AQUA Rich.**

EYE MASK

The secret to getting some serious shuteye on your flight home? This mask, which will help you relax with its yuzu (Japanese citrus fruit) or rose scent.
-> **KAO Megurhythm**

A ROUND OF BEAUTY

Don't forget to exclaim "Kawaii!" followed by an excited little squeal: that's what the Japanese do when they see something that's adorable, innocent, and vulnerable all at the same time. Kawaii is Pikachu and Hello Kitty, pastel colors and rainbows, things that are small, soft, and round – it's cuteness with a capital C and, above all, it's an actual Japanese pop-culture philosophy that is taken very seriously.

KAWAII MONSTER CAFÉ

To start your journey into the world of *kawaii*, teleport yourself directly into the parallel universe of the Kawaii Monster Café, an atmospheric café-cum-entertainment space, complete with costumes, songs, and rainbow-colored food...

Kawaii Monster Café
YM square building 4F, 4-31-10, Jingumae, Shibuya, Tokyo
東京都渋谷区神宮前4-31-10
Lunch: 11:30am / 4:30pm
Dinner: 6pm / 10:30pm
Tel: +81 3-5413-6142
kawaiimonster.jp

RAINBOW COTTON CANDY

Come here, in the Harajuku district of Tokyo, for pastel rainbow-colored cotton candy that's prepared in front of your eyes, adorable little cake-pops

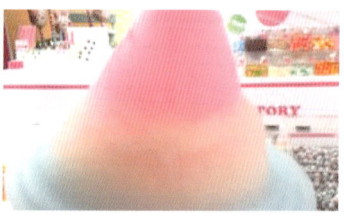

(cake on lollipop sticks), and candy in every shape and color.

Totti Candy Factory
2F, 1-16-5 Jingumae, Shibuya-ku, Tokyo
東京都渋谷区神宮前1-16-5 RYUアパルトマン2F
10:30am / 8pm Saturday
9:30am / 8pm Sunday
Tel: +81 3-3403-7007
www.totticandy.com
(on the uber-kawaii street Takeshita in Harajuku)

DON'T FORGET YOUR IPHONE

In a city that takes its desserts (almost) more seriously than its politics, Dominique Ansel's café is one of the brightest stars on Instagram. It's Dominique Ansel who first crossed croissants with donuts to give us cronuts, and he's also the inventor of corn and watermelon ice cream.

Dominique Ansel Bakery
5-7-14 Jingumae, Shibuya-ku, Tokyo 京都渋谷区神宮前5-7-14
10am / 7pm
Tel: +81 3-3486-1329
www.dominiqueanseljapan.com/

PHOTO CREDIT: @KAWAIIMONSTERCAFE, TOTTICANDYFACTORY, DOMINIQUEANSELBAKERY,

XXXXL ICE CREAM

Anywhere Door is an extremely minimalist boutique with extremely maximalist ice creams, available in a dozen varieties, with cones coated on the inside and decorated on the outside with multicolored sprinkles. Beware: serious risk of overdose.

Anywhere Door
3-27-15 Jingumae, Shibuya-ku, Tokyo
東京都渋谷区神宮前3-27-15 FLAG 1A
11am / 7pm
Tel: +81 3-6721-1995
www.anywheredoor.jp

EAT A COMPLETELY BLUE MEAL

Located in Asakusa, an old district of Tokyo, Kipposhi is a little ramen place that serves soup with chicken that's... completely blue (the color is derived from a mysterious natural ingredient that only the chef knows). Better yet, it's delicious.

Kipposhi
3-1-17 Azumabashi, Sumida, Tokyo
東京都墨田区吾妻橋3-1-17 吾妻橋ハイム101
Lunch: 11:30am / 2:30pm
Dinner: 5:30pm / 9pm
closed on Wednesday
Tel: +81 3-6658-8802

VISIT A CAT TEMPLE

In the Gotokuji district, you'll find this temple dedicated entirely to cats, with hundreds of white cat statues (the inspiration behind the famous maneki-neko, the ubiquitous feline figurine that waves hello with its paw in the air) lined up on an altar, meant to bring you good luck.

Gotokuji
2-24-7 Gotokuji, Setagaya, Tokyo
谷区豪徳寺2-24-7 豪徳寺
9am / 4:30pm
Tel: +81 3-3426-1437

PET AN OWL

With Tokyo apartments being as small as shoeboxes, their occupants don't have a hope of squeezing in a pet. Which explains the popularity of animal cafés, where you can go to pet animals. After bars dedicated to cats, dogs, and rabbits, owl cafés are now where it's at.

Owl Cafe & Bar
1-21-15 Jingumae, Shibuya, Tokyo, Harajuku ATM Bldg. 4F 渋谷区神宮前1-21-15 ATM 4F
11am / 7pm
www.owlvillage.jp
(expect to spend about 2,500 yen, including one drink)

"PURIKURIFY" YOURSELF

There's nothing Japanese kids love more than purikura – taking pictures in a photo booth of sorts that transforms you into a star... Well, the Japanese version of a star, anyway – namely, with a Hello Kitty smile, doe eyes, and an elongated body. You can even choose virtual makeup and customize your pictures with kawaii icons. Want even more? Well, you can have it: Japanese schoolgirl, waitress, and unicorn costumes are available for rent.

Calla Lily
Shibuya Chitose Kaikan Bldg. 1F, 13-8, Udagawacho, Shibuya-ku
渋谷区宇田川町13-8 渋谷ちとせ会館
11am / 11:30pm
Tel: +81 3-5784-0280

PHOTO CREDIT: @ANYWHEREDOOR_JP, SIBASAKI1001

MANY THANKS TO

AURÉLIE R, for being the first to introduce Fany to Tokyo.

IKUMI, for accompanying her on all her explorations and for the 1,001 incredible strings she pulled for us.

IWONKA, for ferreting out priceless spots, investigating unheard-of places, managing to fit "round pegs in square holes," and for all the sake-fueled belly laughs.

AKO, for introducing us to so many amazing people and for translating the craziest conversations.

OUSSAMA, or getting up to no good with us in Japan.

KANAKO, AURÉLIE S AND FABIAN, for retranscribing the soul of this city in pictures and drawings.

THOMAS, our expedition leader.

This book was created by:

Fany and Amandine Péchiodat,
co-founders of My Little Paris, authors

Iwonka Bancerek, local scout and blogger,
follow her on Instragram on @toteone

Kanako Kuno, illustrator
Fabian Parkes, photographer
Aurélie Saint-Martin, artistic director and layout design
Emmanuelle Willard Toulemonde, layout
Sophie Schlondorff, translation
Jana Gough, editing
Eleni Salemi, proofreading
Clémence Mathé, publishing

You can write to us at contact@soul-of-cities.com
Follow us on Instagram on @soul_of_guides

In accordance with regularly upheld French jurisprudence (Toulouse 14-01-1887), the publisher will not be deemed responsible for any involuntary errors or omissions that may subsist in this guide despite our diligence and verifications by the editorial staff.
Any reproduction of the content, or part of the content, of this book by whatever means is forbidden without prior authorization by the publisher.

© JONGLEZ 2018
Registration of copyright: October 2018 - Edition: 01
ISBN: 978-2-36195-290-7
Printed in Bulgaria by Multiprint